# IF THIS SHOULD REACH YOU IN TIME

## JUSTIN MARKS

**BARRELHOUSE BOOKS**

Published by Barrelhouse Books
Baltimore, Maryland
www.barrelhousemag.com

Published in the United States of America
ISBN 13: 979-8-9850089-1-3

First Edition
Cover art and book design by Shanna Compton

*In memoriam*
*Peter J. Rohana Jr.*

# CONTENTS

# AN INCANTATION

What the poem calls for

is trust    A lack

of fear    A politics

of love    Resistance    Layers

of previous selves

peeled away

No answers    No desire

for control    It knows

nothing about you

Doesn't give a fuck

What it wants

is your love    Your scorn

To love you    To leave you

different    What it gives

is choice    Sense

and nonsense    Doubt

and faith and naivety

The poem is

a revolutionary

A mind that keeps moving

after the body dies

The brain that knows

it's dead   Musicians playing

their instruments so well

it doesn't look real

What the poem does is nothing

except ask that you sit

in its words   Inhabit them

Their sounds   Sit

and be still   Let

whatever happens, happen

It's dark

What light there is

is blurry

You're a child

Someone is explaining

the Cold War

Someone is telling you

about nuclear bombs

You're scared, terrified

to be precise

Awareness of death

That's not new

Aware of death and scared

That's new

An inauguration

of fear that ignites

in you an urgency

without object

Isolation    In time

at a religious service

though you're not religious

you'll come to a part

in a prayer that says

*Around us is life and death*

*decay and renewal*

*The flowing rhythm that all things obey*

A part in a prayer that says

*Our life is a dance to a song*

*we cannot hear*

A part in a prayer that says

*Its melody courses through us*

*for a little while then seems to cease*

A part in a prayer that says

*Lord what are we*

A part in a prayer that says

*A breath, a passing shadow*

A part in a prayer that says

*Yet you have made us*

*little less than divine*

You will feel something

Call it a connection

Peace, calm

The world is hopeless

You know that

but will feel hope

You will feel hope

and find a voice

You will find a voice

and rise

You will rise

and take action

But that is many

broken worlds away

# SOME THINGS MIGHT BE WORTH TELLING
# SIMPLY BECAUSE THEY'RE HAPPENING
### (a variation on a line by Maggie Nelson)

It's cold

like those childhood winters when

the temperature got so low

outside it hurt to breathe

but lacking any other choice

you took your next breath, your next

step toward whatever future lay ahead

Whatever state    Only now the cold hurts more

inflicts a pain that can only be described

as spiritual    *All systems fail eventually*

you say to yourself, as if that were adequate

explanation    As if that could prepare you

for what's next    For what you can barely

begin to imagine

# BELIEF AND NAÏVETY

The face is a template of which
there are only so many versions

A country we no longer recognize
that is the country we've always recognized

but pretended we didn't
Our greatest sin

Anger that sustains itself with anger
about being angry

The ruin we inflict on the world
getting in the way

of the ruin we further seek
to inflict on the world

Dark highways illuminated
by hills on fire

The light in me
that is the light in you

that is the light
in all of us

A name
A memory

Heartbreak from which
there is no recovery

# ALONG FOR THE RIDE

There's no way around
not being part

of the problem
Innovations in war

The creation of what
we were supposed to prevent

Assume the body doesn't feel
anything in particular

The sun falling behind
the sea   An overwhelming

sense of urgency   It's OK
to not remember things

To take it all at face value
until it's not

The best case scenario
is long term disaster

Gutted deer
hanging from barn rafters

Angels watching
indifferently

# ON THE 50<sup>TH</sup> ANNIVERSARY OF THE FIRST LUNAR LANDING

Homecoming queens

practice their pageant waves

on the backs of convertibles

in a church parking lot

✦

I fall

Break a bone

Pain like pain is all

there's been or will be

Something just beyond sight, lurking

or obvious explanation

A metal plate holds

my bone together

✦

Low clouds rise

like mountains over

the still waters

of the small bay

at dusk

●

"I got to my unit the day before. The day of Tet we went to the US embassy then wound up at a bridge. Two weeks there and thought I would never make it. Lots of action. Had same clothes on for two weeks. Slept on the bridge. No bathroom, just shit on the bridge. I was feet away when that famous photo was taken of the police chief shooting the VC prisoner in the head. It was a major adjustment from college to war."

●

Hunger awakens hunger

An expanse of sea

Future psychedelic

states of utopia

●

We're the masters

of our own destruction

Convergence and

dysfunction

●

"Our grandma was from Latvia. She used to make us sing, 'God Bless America' and wave tiny flags before we sat down to eat at family gatherings. My uncles would gamble and pass out. Die young. Someone would get the horse's ass

award. They'd be given a small statue of a horse's ass. The
story is grandpa was a horse thief back in the old country.
Sometimes we'd play softball, schlemiels VS schlimazels.
When my brother came home from the war, we had a party.
Grandma tore off his uniform and stomped on it."

◆

The old order is dead

The new hasn't

been determined

A code that's the words themselves

Volatile energy

◆

"I was just back from the war when we landed on the moon.
I was starting back at college that week and bought a 16 inch
black and white TV. It was such a major accomplishment.
Everyone was so excited. They showed the landing and the
crowds cheering in Times Square. It restored confidence in
our country. The war was tearing us apart."

◆

The crowd chants

Send her back

Send her back

Send her back

Words reluctantly

disavowed

A disavowal

disavowed

❧

How does a thing feel

not to an observer-perceiver but

to the thing itself

Perhaps like nothing

Most likely

nothing

Except the thing

inherent in nothing

Its inverse presence

A united state

❧

"It was such a confusing time. I'd go to war protests, but also my brother was over there. I was against the war but not against him. He'd send letters home. The ones that came to our house were mainly about how hot and boring it was. 'I'm safe,' he'd say, 'not a lot going on here.' Those were for our mother.

The others were addressed to me and dad and sent to dad's work address. In those, my brother talked about how much action he was seeing, friends dying, how scared he was he might not make it home. How the light the flares traced across the sky over his base camp at night were actually kind of beautiful.

The last protest I went to the crowd was chanting about how the soldiers were baby killers. A friend I was with—she knew my brother was over there—she was chanting it too, looked right at me and chanted that. I...I just didn't know what to do. It was such a confusing time."

◆

I'm looking through

old pictures from

sixth grade graduation of me

and my friends

with our mullets

and clothes for special occasions

from K-Mart

I'm the only one

left alive

Why me

I wonder

more as a formality

a thing to think because

I'm unsure

of anything else

what to feel or say, who

if anyone

to share it with

or even how much

I care

It's sad

That was

a long time ago

I made it out

of that town

those days

of pain and alienation

of wanting to be anything

but who I

woke up and

went to sleep as

spent my days

hating

That person is gone

those friends and that time

I'm here

The days still arriving

The heat and diseases

fires and floods

Hunger awakening hunger

# IF THIS SHOULD REACH YOU IN TIME

If this should reach you in time know
that we didn't see

the disaster coming

That it wasn't
imaginable, hadn't

existed until, gradually
it was, and did

Or that we saw it
and refused to believe

Or saw it and thought
something or someone

else would save us

Or, as in some Hollywood disaster movie
we'd set aside

our differences, rise

to the occasion and save
ourselves    Save you

from what we created
but didn't

and now can only offer
our sincerest and not quite

empty apologies

◆

If this should reach you in time
know that we knew about it all—

the advent of our species
as a geological force

earthquakes that cause
tsunamis and volcanoes

volcanoes and earthquakes
that cause tsunamis

changes in climate that lead
to increases in all three

tidal flooding
and water shortages

dams about to burst
and wash away

cities of millions
the multiple and

interacting causes
of death we caused

The problem was different
people wanted different things

The problem was nobody
had answers

The problem
was us

❧

But we did try
some of us

to do what we could
Some more than others

But even when what we could do
was momentous and great

it wasn't enough

At times we made jokes

Attempts to reclaim
the goodness of laughter

from the insanity
of market logic

to combat
the reality of being less

alive every day
The unstoppable processes

set in motion
Future consequences

already locked in
The new language

of fires and floods
diseases and extinctions

we were learning
The incompatibility

of capitalism
with our survival

We were empowered
but powerless

Resistant but
because powerless

compliant
Life continued

The trips to the gym
and grocery store

Days at work
Vacations

Evenings at home

New hairstyles and catchy
pop songs

Our phones in our pockets

Occasionally
we'd see it clearly

The accumulation
of (un)intended consequences

Casualties and carnage
enormous and unmeasured

War
forever

Power
consolidated

Constant crisis
the dominant mode

Crisis
curation

for maximum
profit

The network of artificial
instincts we call tradition

Gunships gathering
overhead

◆

No one is safe
The future is

lives spent fleeing
and recovering

from catastrophe
Volcanic ash and moisture

mixing in the air
to fill our lungs

with a kind of pulmonary cement
Heat waves thawing

frozen wastes
causing deadly

outbreaks of dormant disease
We knew

and let it happen
Knew it was

too late

We were
already dead

If this should reach you
know that the people were

incapable of
resolving differences

That the best
we could hope for

was to be wrong
in our separate and intractable

apocalyptic
visions of the future

Our anger toward
each other

Distrust

Masses of birds fly for miles
in the eyes of hurricanes

surrounded on all sides
by wind and thunderstorms

Yet, because they're in the middle of the storm
they're sheltered from it

No such thing
can be said of us

◆

If this should reach
you in time

know that the ultimate
vengeance is forgiveness

That we're sorry
We're so so sorry

◆

Our worst selves

it turns out
are our true selves

A wildfire spreading

Zero percent
contained

◆

That we are inherently
selfish and self-

destructive is
an obvious

conclusion to come to
Yet is all

I can come to
Time goes by

slow
and then

it doesn't
The falseness of a thing

that makes it real

◆

What will be left:
A crust roamed

by what animals remain
An approximation

of eternity

◆

What we can say is
we left you

things to look back on
Stories

of questionable consolation
The infinite beauty

of futile acts
of defiance

People who
keep living

# I HAVE NO IDEA WHAT'S GOING TO HAPPEN

I wanted to be home

but stopped instead

and sat on a bench

I sat for a long time

not really thinking

though thoughts would

come and go

I wasn't looking

at anything in particular either

I was watching

It was March

Still cold, foggy

Had been raining

An older man sang

in Spanish to a woman

walking next to him

The woman joined him in song

eventually

And then they laughed

and talked

I understood

none of it

but in the silence reborn

after they passed

I sat

The fog began receding

I'm still sitting there

Waiting

## DOING MORE IS NEVER ENOUGH
*(ending with a variation on a line by Nicanor Parra)*

There is no time
Only experience

A certain off-
balance quality

A word breaks loose
A room gains depth

Then is
a plain room again

Some of us just
waking up

Some of us
awake already

Every good thing we do
Every bad thing

As if there were
nothing wrong in America

# A SONG IS JUST A SUGGESTION FOR WHAT CAN HAPPEN

Thoughts are problems

when you can't

stop thinking about them

I can't

stop thinking about

how my thoughts

are more like sensations

nice dreams about

something I can't remember

The wisdom of parents

with no

wisdom to offer

I hear a voice

assume it's speaking to me

Misread *shellfish*

as *selfish*

and let that

speak for itself

An exercise

in humility

Magical

emotions

My mind gone

completely blank

# WATCHING THE RIVER FLOW, THE TRAFFIC GO BY

A world that almost was
matters as much as one that is

The picture not
taken the word
left silent

What we want
from people is
rarely what we get

Signals we're not
conscious of
passing between us

Is it weird to say
how much I enjoy
being polite

Courtesy and certain
formalities

Diminished
irreverence

Like noticing the first
time you don't
notice something amazing

As if the purpose of writing
is to exhaust
the urge to write

The enormous
impossible power
I placed in words

A good song
I wish was better

## WHY BE SPARING IN PRAISE

So little matters

You solve a problem
Create another

The work that never stops
A slip

while walking
that jars the whole body

As if there were some
inherent purpose to that

Stars aligned
we'll never know

A higher power
called magic

Zero regard
for the mind's disorder

## PERSONAL BEST

I hate talking

I talk so much

I no longer have a voice

I look at the past

and feel distance

I tell my therapist

I want to take up

as little space as possible

I tell my inner monologue

to just stop already

*Tell me more,* my therapist says

*How's anybody gonna get to heaven*

*if nobody wants to die*

a stranger yells

The escalators are broken

Consciousness is energy spent

between ourselves

and others

is a phrase I recently shared with a friend

A conception of movement on our bodies

that we transfer to others

A layer of language between direct experience

and the external record of it

*I'll have to think about that*

my friend said

What would it feel like to be free

of whatever dictates this dread and discomfort

No idea

so I put the point in the presentation

for you to consider

I listen

and the pain is less

There's a purpose

Interruption as often as possible

Butter that makes every bite of bread better

Phrases there's little reason to share

but I share nonetheless

as an invitation—

an invocation—

to and of openness

the subtle and sudden swerves

of nuance and dialogue

A song we make up as we go along

An ever-present melody

we say into existence

Observation and wonder

A thing we share—

overwhelming in its ordinariness—

and then move on

Practice without performance

Innuendos that appear and disappear

Practice as performance

The difference is perception

Meaning that decays over time

and leaves us less

and more ourselves

Promise unfulfilled

The ending still

unsung

## AGING OUT

I'm not good

with disruption

Most mornings

I read poems

Evenings too

Demons in the doorway

waiting to be born

Angels about

to enter

Shame is worthless

Fucked up

is the only way

I used to know to be

Now I just let the elevators

take me wherever

Ghosts gliding

between the lines

Bird embryos communicating

through vibrations

Songs I've loved and forgotten

their long notes held

just so

Peace and exultation

Hits and misses

Misery is certain

The sin of freedom is

how we use it

against others

The long consequences

of a single act

Aggressively positive

T-shirt slogans

A lot lately

I catch myself whispering

*It doesn't matter*

to no one in particular

by which I suspect I mean

*My body is making progress*

*My bones are getting brittle*

Something like that

It doesn't matter

My existence

is little

A long

healthy life

Nowhere near

healed

## ALL I USED TO WANT WAS YOUR ATTENTION

I'm not good
with emojis

To believe a thing is real
I need to hear it
repeatedly—

the multiple narratives
unspooling simultaneously

ongoing scandals

an old friend continuing
to drink himself to death

It will always be
and not
be real

My desire to be right
is almost zero

A body
of work

Broken
concentration

All the wound care
questions answered

*Aging,* says my chiropractor,
*is the process of your body*
*slowly drying up,*

*cells depleting*
*each time they divide*

A living record
of my demise

The fragile peace
of a happy home

# BELIEF ITSELF IS FULFILLMENT

The more present I become

the more something else

disappears

Each terrible thing waiting

to happen anew

An unknown problem

of no one's making

making itself

known

◆

I lose my balance

My shadow leans

toward the light

The intimidating sky

Stable points

of reference

◆

A set of circumstances

and faith in a not

awful outcome

Abstinence

that makes the heart

grow fonder

A world that's broken

but works anyway

Its incomprehensible clatter

◆

Sometimes I hear the last words

of people who aren't dead yet

and they are devastating

Sometimes all I hear

is ringing

My failure to keep pace

with my ambition

My immense ignorance

Light reflecting

off fresh snow

## ALL I WANT IS TO FEEL PREPARED

I used to want poems
to destroy me

fill me with sadness
that makes me feel alive

Now I want them
to put me back together

Reveal the un-
reality of being

Encode in me not
comfort with it

but the exquisite resolve of
brokenness survived

## WHO'S SPEAKING NOW

Every story

is a false story

A glance

in the mirror

Infinite

scroll

Genuine emotion

followed by

crushing guilt

Good that's not

necessarily

enough

The reflection

is a construct

# THE SCAR ON MY WRIST IS NOT WHAT YOU THINK

Expectation

is disappointment

I try not to look

like I look

This person

who's not

that person

anymore

This knot

that's not

going to hold

# THE APPEARING ACT

I doze

Don't know where

or who

I am

These out

of context utterances

I utter

My un-

inviting vibe

People caring for each other

in panicked ways

# SING ALONG

The hereditary is here

An ecosystem

burning   Fish circling

our legs as we wade

in clear water

on the pristine shore

of an empty beach

A metal cleat spiked

into an outcrop of rock

for mooring a boat

The uncertain outcome

of antagonistic forces

We want everything

to be fine

so say it will be

and hope for the best

People drinking without any

apparent intention

of getting drunk

The music isn't

fragile

The memory is real

Its pre-nostalgia

Dark and golden wings

Reasonable

paranoia

There's nothing to be afraid of

I say

and think I might

actually mean it

The only people we have

are ourselves

A question to which

I have no answer

A bridge empties
into a cliff

An act without
fear of punishment

hope
of reward

A parrot capable
of kindness

My anger
was my talent

a knack for
a furious rant

A song
of loss

in-
significance

A bridge empties
into the face

of a cliff
A softened look

Such joy
so easily

forgotten

# LONE FIGURES AT A DISTANCE

The birds I like
are all the birds

you're not supposed to like
Married couples awkwardly kissing

An argument among thoughts
in an undecided mind

Physical contact
at a distance

Devotion
and struggle

A child gently placing
a package on a shelf

Normal occurrence
Unexpected

mood
Hands chapped

from so much
scrubbing

◆

Abandoned subways
Abandoned streets

Feral cats occupying
ancient ruins

All we had to do
was that which

we weren't capable of
A company about to go

panic    I mean
public

My spiritual condition
isn't awesome

I feel safest
when my phone

is fully charged

Vitamins
in my veins

My routine
is erratic

The ocean is
off-limits

A fire that holds
my attention

Seashells crushed
underfoot

Constellations
dying

If you have to explain the joke
it's even funnier

❖

It hurts

this home
that is confinement

Sleep
and waking

Openness
and desperation

Work continuing
at its diminished pace

◆

Sadness and absurdity
beauty and joy

Bodily feelings observed
from positions of

nonidentification
Rivers emptied

of all vessels
Intimacy a distant

country
I will always want

there to be more
to say

I will always hear
accusations

in the most
benign utterances

Monetized
decisions and missed

opportunities for gentleness
Escape

from suffering and other
impossibilities

Yellow leaves falling back
onto trees

I'm here
muscles sore

I sit
in a chair

Lay
in bed

Each day a new
form of dread

Days once being
all we had

Now not
even that

The world united
in fear

of illness
fragility

and repetition
Chords casually strummed

drifting into
lost song

Years back I biked
out to Corson's Inlet

in homage to Archie Ammons
or just for some exercise

Wrote a few lines
about the gulls arcing out

over the inlet
that went nowhere

but I have carried
ever since

The overcast sky
Hood of my hoodie

half over my head
Kids playing catch

on the silent shore
A quaintness, almost

innocence to it all
Presence slipping

into absence

◆

I stay up
and write

Make long
playlists

of sad songs

Each one
an elegy

New rhythm
of loss

and perseverance
Cycles of

suppression
and lift

Maybe even
nostalgia

for something
changing so fast

nostalgia itself
is lost

like everything else

we struggle
to keep

◆

At night I forget
where I am

and walk
into walls

My phone fails
to recognize

my face

◆

Lines
and movement

Energy

The need to speak
Not much to say

◆

Shut down
the shutdown

the protesters say
unmasked

gathered at
reckless distances

❧

I walk in whatever
direction

No closer
to better

I had a vision for myself
The vision failed

Who's speaking is no longer
clear

The vast ocean
Violent waves

How is it with you
stranger

It takes it out of you
this life occupying

a body
Inconsistent and contradictory

Wasted on anxiety and withdrawal
from medication

A system operating at maximum
reduced capacity

I've lost track
of the conversation

◆

At night someone wakes me and says
don't breathe

My friends
your beloved names

escape me
The breeze and whatever

it does
I'm already

unprepared
We're already

no longer here

To be in need of relief and know
there is no relief

To know each day
has never meant so much as now

That these days are the end
and beginning—

a duality that is only
part of the pain

To be at a point of such loss
there are no words

The loss
compounds

The lack
gains urgency

until you don't
break exactly

but plod on
under a weight

you're certain
you can no longer

bear
and then

bear

Eager to see
what happens

I miss
what happens

The threat my
identity poses

My ego
Inadequate and worn

Writing toward a clarity
I move further from

with each
word

What feels different
isn't

A lost sense
of family

◆

Something's dying

I'm sick

of my vocabulary

Defaults and habits

of mind    The way

I walk    What I want

is to put into words

my own silence

A mess of text

I can't help

but make

◆

The timelines don't align

The basic assumption is impossibility

The threat of America

The notion of nations

The speed and agility of a fighter jet

minus the lethal intent

History gets longer

The experiment fails

The high school football team

staggers onto the field

A sunset on another planet

The distance is vast

Preparation is key

Waves washing away

a newly built beach

•

Nothing matters and then it does

There's a plan and then there isn't

Vague image called a vision

The music of the dead

Their singing   Its jarring

rhythms   Discordant

melody   There is no

security   Ideas form

then crumble   Call it

history   A child stung

by a bee   The child

screams   Wants somebody

to do something   Nobody

does   Call it knowledge

That which is there

regardless of belief

Odd phrases

Conspicuous absences

The illusion is real   A timeline

of circumstance bending in a direction

to be determined

◆

A freighter floats down

the otherwise undisturbed

Hudson    Time slows

to a smudge

Not wanting to sleep

but wanting to sleep

Then takes distinct shape again

What is happening

has consequences

Impassable

hours    Lost

travelers

◆

This is unpublishable
I say to a friend

As in, not meant to be
or not thinking about

publication
Some poems

all they want
is to be published

Though I admit
I'm lost as to what

poetry could possibly be
if not

emptiness shared
among friends

I fear I'll never
see again

## A PRAYER

The season refuses

to abandon us

Crooked features

of my face

Skin losing

its elastic

We get sad

Move on

Billionaires bet

on futures markets

in human behavior

The words prey

and predator

Each breath

a passing shadow

How we all gather

at different rivers

What I want

is to celebrate

revel in the immense

joy of

a simple shift

in focus—

long conversation

in a park

with a good friend

I haven't seen in months

as the light moves

from dusk to dark

and the trees

and buildings tower

and other people go about

doing I assume the same

and a child's toy car sits

abandoned on the lawn

## ACKNOWLEDGMENTS

Grateful acknowledgment to publications in which versions of these poems first appeared: *Conjunctions*, the *Inquisitive Eater* and *Iterant*.

Thanks to Sampson Starkweather and Chris Tonelli for reading this manuscript many times over and providing thoughtful, caring and compassionate feedback, insight and encouragement.

Eternal love and gratitude to Meri, Louisa and Henry—my hearts, my world.

Thanks to my editor, Dan Brady, and the Barrelhouse team for their time, care, attention and generosity in the process of making this book a reality.

# ABOUT THE AUTHOR

Justin Marks's books are, *If This Should Reach You in Time* (Barrelhouse Books, 2022), *The Comedown* (Publishing Genius Press, 2021), *You're Going to Miss Me When You're Bored* (Barrelhouse Books, 2014), and *A Million in Prizes* (New Issues, 2009). He is a cofounder of Birds, LLC, an independent poetry press, and lives in New York City with his family.

www.ingramcontent.com/pod-product-compliance
Lightning Source LLC
Chambersburg PA
CBHW030851090426
42737CB00009B/1182